The Veiled Architect

# SECRET

# MONEY

# DOMINATION

Steal the Wealth Strategies of the 1%
and Break Free from Financial Slavery

Staton House

1

*Written in silence.*

*Forged in resistance.*

*Released for those who refuse to die obedient.*

# Table of Contents

# Introduction – The Hidden Game of Wealth

## Why Hard Work Doesn't Equal Riches

You were sold a dream.
Get up early. Stay late. Be a team player. Grind it out for 40 years.
Then maybe—just maybe—you'll retire with a little dignity.

**Let me rip the mask off that lie.**

Hard work isn't what makes people rich. If it did, coal miners would be billionaires, single moms working double shifts would own mansions, and janitors would have private jets.

But they don't. You know who does?

People who control assets. People who use leverage. People who move capital like chess pieces. People who don't trade their time—they trade **your time.**

This lie was engineered to keep you obedient. Because if you believe that working harder will fix your money problems, you won't ask bigger questions. You won't learn the real game. You'll just grind until you break.

And when you burn out? They'll replace you. Quietly. Without a thank you.

### The Lie Has a Purpose

Think about who benefits from this fantasy:

- Employers get loyal, compliant workers.

- Banks get borrowers for life.

- The government gets predictable tax cattle.

- Universities get lifetime debt slaves.

- The rich? They get richer—off the back of your labor.

**The lie isn't random. It's strategic.**

They've built a machine that runs on your energy—but will never give you equity.

You're told to save. But inflation devours your savings.
You're told to buy a house. But you end up a mortgage prisoner.
You're told to invest in a 401(k). But the real wealth is in private deals and asymmetric bets you're locked out of.

This isn't just unfair. It's war.

**And hard work is the weapon they use against you.**

**What the Rich Do Instead**

The rich understand something you weren't taught:
**It's not about effort. It's about position.**

They position themselves to:

- **Own**, not rent.

- **Receive**, not labor.

- **Multiply**, not trade time.

- **Access**, not apply.

They acquire assets that print money whether they're sleeping, traveling, or ignoring their emails.

They build systems that scale their income.

They protect that wealth using legal armor—while the average person prays for a raise.

**Here's the Brutal Truth:**

If you're still trading time for money as your *main* strategy, you're losing a rigged game.
If you're still believing hard work is the answer, you're living inside the matrix they built for you.

And that ends now.

This book will expose how the system really works, how the 1% rigged it, and how to steal back the strategies they've hidden from you.

Because freedom doesn't come from hustle. It comes from **leverage**.

And leverage comes from **truth**.

# What You Were Never Taught About Money

You were never meant to be rich.

If that stings, good. Because until you accept it, you'll keep chasing freedom using tools designed to **trap** you.

Ask yourself:
Why did you spend 12+ years in school—and not one hour learning how money actually works?

Why can you recite the Pythagorean theorem, but not explain how a mortgage traps you in 30 years of financial slavery?

Why are you told to "budget and save," but not taught how the rich use debt, entities, and tax codes to multiply wealth while paying almost nothing?

**Because they don't want you free.**
They want you dependent.
Grateful.
Tame.

## Schools Were Never About Wealth—They're About Compliance

Your school didn't fail you.
**It performed exactly as designed.**

The modern school system was built during the Industrial Revolution—to create compliant workers for factories. Not owners. Not rebels. Not thinkers.

They taught you to sit still, raise your hand, follow orders, and accept the grade you're given.

Sound familiar?

It's the same structure your job follows. The same hierarchy. The same illusion of progress. And just like school, **it punishes independence**.

That's not a coincidence.
That's engineering.

### What the Elite Teach Their Own

While you were being trained to obey, **the wealthy were learning to dominate.**

Here's what they pass down to their children:

- **Money is a game of strategy, not effort.**
- **Wealth is built in private, not public markets.**
- **Taxes are rules for the uninformed.**
- **Control is more important than ownership.**

They teach their kids how to think in terms of **leverage, capital movement**, and **protection.** You were taught how to write a résumé.

They learn how to build *entities* and *networks*. You learned how to ask for time off.

This is not an accident. It's a class firewall.
And financial illiteracy is the lock that keeps you out.

### Ignorance is the Real Currency of Control

Think about who wins when you don't know how money works:

- Banks win: You borrow, they print.
- Governments win: You earn, they tax.
- Employers win: You trade time, they keep scale.

11

- Asset owners win: You rent, they get rich.

But you? You're stuck hustling in a system that was built to extract your time, energy, and dreams—**forever.**

And the more confused you are about how the game works, the less likely you are to challenge it.

So they keep you busy. Distracted. Overstimulated. Under-informed.

You were trained to survive in a system they *never intended you to escape.*

But knowledge is the key.
And now you've got the lockpick.

In the next section, we're going to lay it all bare. You'll see **exactly how the system is built to keep you poor**, and why the rat race isn't just real—it's rigged.

# Why the System Is Built to Keep You Poor

You didn't stumble into financial struggle.
You were **guided** into it—step by step.

From the moment you could walk, you were groomed to play a very specific role: **producer, payer, prisoner.**

Let's break it down.

## 1. The Education–Debt–Job Pipeline

From kindergarten to college, you were marched through a system with one goal: make you "employable."

Not financially literate.
Not sovereign.
**Employable.**

Here's the formula they fed you:

- Go to school.

- Take on debt for college.

- Get a "good" job.

- Work 40+ years.

- Retire (maybe) if you're lucky.

This isn't a life plan—it's **a debt trap disguised as opportunity**.

By 18, you're encouraged to sign your name to $50,000+ in student loans… without a single financial education class.

Think about that.

The system won't let you rent a car at 18, but it will legally chain you to decades of compound debt with zero training. That's not incompetence—it's **intentional design.**

Once you graduate, guess what?

You're so desperate to pay it off that you'll accept **any job**. And just like that, you're plugged in. Taxed, tracked, and too tired to question it.

## 2. Inflation, Taxation, and Silent Theft

Even if you play their game "correctly"—work hard, budget, save—**the system still robs you blind.**

How?

- **Inflation**: Every year, your money buys less. Prices go up. Your salary doesn't. The dollar dies slowly—and silently.

- **Taxation**: Your biggest lifetime expense. The more you earn from labor, the more they take. Meanwhile, the rich earn from *assets*—and pay less (or nothing).

- **Depreciating money**: They print more currency. You lose purchasing power. They call it "stimulus." It's really legalized theft.

If you saved $10,000 in the bank ten years ago, congratulations: it's worth significantly less today. That's the magic trick of fiat money.

You don't feel the robbery because it's spread out over decades. But make no mistake—you're being drained.

## 3. The 9-to-5 Loop Is a Cage

Here's the dirtiest truth:
**Jobs are not designed to make you rich.**

They are designed to keep you:

- **Busy enough not to rebel**

- **Comfortable enough not to leave**

- **Dependent enough not to question**

The 40-hour week doesn't exist because it's efficient—it exists because it **exhausts you just enough** to kill your dreams, but not your productivity.

It leaves no space for freedom-building:

- No time to study wealth.

- No bandwidth to launch assets.

- No energy to build leverage.

You clock in, you pay your bills, and you start over. Forever.

They've even rigged the language:

- "Good job" = loyalty to the system.

- "Stable income" = capped income.

- "Benefits" = golden handcuffs.

And worst of all?

If you try to leave the matrix, **people will call you crazy**. They'll tell you to be grateful. That fear is another part of the trap.

**The System Wins When You Stay Small**

Understand this:

- They don't care about your potential.

- They don't care how hard you work.

- They don't care how good you are.

They care that you **stay in your place**.

Because if you ever break free, stop trading time for money, and start owning income-producing assets, **you become competition.**

And the system does not reward competition from outsiders.

The system is a machine.
Your poverty is the fuel.
And your freedom is the threat.

But now you see it. And once you see the bars, you can escape the cage.

# What's Inside This Book—and How to Use It

Now that you've seen the trap, it's time to learn how to **break it.**

This isn't a book about "thinking positive," budgeting apps, or drinking less coffee. That's what they give the masses to **distract** them.

What you're holding is **financial contraband**—the real playbook used by the wealthy to create untouchable freedom.

Here's what you're about to uncover:

**Chapter 1 –** *The Financial Prison*

You'll see how the system was built—from education to inflation to taxation—to keep you trapped. Once you see the prison, you'll stop playing the inmate.

**Chapter 2 –** *Secrets of the 1%*

We break down the tools and philosophies the elite actually use. Trusts, LLCs, private banking, "own nothing, control everything"—this is how power is built and protected.

**Chapter 3 –** *Wealth Myths That Keep You Broke*

From "saving your way to wealth" to "buying a house is an investment," we destroy the mainstream lies that keep you poor and obedient.

**Chapter 4 –** *Secret Loopholes of the Rich*

How they legally pay no taxes. How they use debt as fuel. How they hide income and protect assets. These aren't conspiracy theories—they're open secrets **they hope you never learn.**

## Chapter 5 – *Hidden Financial Moves You Were Never Meant to See*

From geo-arbitrage to crypto, off-grid income to value storage—you'll learn how to move money outside the matrix and build sovereignty.

## Chapter 6 – *Multiplying Income Without Working Harder*

This is the power of scale. You'll learn how the rich multiply income using systems, automation, and leverage—not effort.

## Chapter 7 – *The Inner Game of Money Domination*

Because domination isn't just tactical—it's psychological. We'll rewire how you think about risk, wealth, and control.

## Final Chapter – *Exit the System: Your Plan to Dominate*

This is where it all comes together. You'll map your exit plan. Design your own wealth machine. Learn how to live free, build untouchable wealth, and **never be owned again.**

---

This isn't a feel-good book. It's a **field manual for financial rebellion.**

Every page will challenge what you've been told. Every chapter will expose what they've hidden. Every tactic is designed for one thing:

**To help you escape the system—and dominate the money game they never wanted you to play.**

You're no longer a worker. You're no longer a pawn.
You're about to become something far more dangerous:

**Informed. Armed. Unstoppable.**

# Chapter 1 – The Financial Prison: How the System Was Built to Trap You

## The Education–Debt–Job Pipeline

They called it the "path to success."

You were told:

- Go to school.

- Get good grades.

- Get into college.

- Take on debt if you have to.

- Graduate.

- Get a job.

- Work hard.

- Retire happy.

That was the script.

But here's the truth they never printed in the brochure:

**That path wasn't built to set you free. It was built to keep you in line.**

**Step 1: Program the Worker**

From the moment you enter school, you're being shaped—not educated. Conditioned to obey bells, follow authority, memorize, repeat, conform.

It's not about critical thinking. It's about **compliance**.

You're not being trained to lead. You're being trained to *submit*. To wait your turn. To need permission. To crave approval.

By the time you're 18, you've been programmed for a world where your value is measured by **grades, credentials, and job titles**— not ownership, not creativity, not freedom.

**Step 2: Trap You in Debt Before You Even Begin**

Then comes the big pitch: college.

You're told it's the golden ticket. But the price? Tens—sometimes hundreds—of thousands of dollars.

And what do they offer in exchange? A piece of paper. No guarantee. No refund. Just a credential in a system that's already **oversaturated and outdated.**

They won't lend you $10,000 to start a business—but they'll lend you $100,000 for a degree that doesn't even guarantee employment.

That's not education. That's **financial onboarding into a lifetime of dependence.**

Most people graduate broke, buried in interest, and desperate to pay it off.

So what happens next?

**Step 3: The Job Hook**

You enter the job market—not because you're passionate or inspired—but because **you're financially cornered.**

You'll take anything. Accept anything. And the system knows it.

This is the most brilliant part of the trap:

**They make you pay to enter a game that immediately owns your time.**

Suddenly, you're stuck in the loop:

- Rent or mortgage.

- Student loan payments.

- Car payment.

- Taxes.

- Insurance.

- Groceries.

- Repeat.

You can't stop. You can't slow down. You're locked in—and you think that's just "being an adult."

But what it really is… is the **prison you were never meant to see.**

And even when you try to get ahead—get a raise, get promoted, climb the ladder—it doesn't change the game. It just makes the cage look nicer.

Because you're still trading time.
You're still paying taxes at the highest rate.
And you're still working inside **someone else's system.**

This is how the 1% designed it.

### The Real Function of the Pipeline

This education–debt–job conveyor belt wasn't built for freedom.

It was built to:

- **Create predictable, tax-paying workers.**

- **Ensure debt-dependent compliance.**

- **Feed profits to banks and corporations.**

- **Prevent rebellion through exhaustion and fear.**

And worst of all?

**They made it look like safety.**

That's the genius.
They didn't put bars around you—they gave you a cubicle and told you to be grateful.

But now that you see it, you can't unsee it.

# Inflation, Taxation, and Silent Theft

The prison doesn't just lock you in. It bleeds you dry.

Not with chains—but with numbers.
Not with violence—but with **systems that quietly rob you every single day.**

Let's start with the dirtiest weapon in their arsenal: **inflation.**

---

### Inflation: The Invisible Pickpocket

You're told that inflation is "normal." Just part of a healthy economy.

But here's the truth:

**Inflation is a hidden tax that steals your purchasing power—and hands it to the elites.**

Every year, the cost of living goes up… but your paycheck doesn't.

Groceries. Gas. Rent. Insurance. Tuition. All climbing.
Meanwhile, your savings? **Losing value while it sits.**

This isn't a natural phenomenon. It's **engineered.**

Governments and central banks print money out of thin air—trillions of dollars—and inject it into the system. That devalues the dollars already in circulation.

And who benefits?

- Asset holders (stocks, real estate, businesses).

- The wealthy, who borrow cheap money and buy appreciating assets.

- Governments, who inflate away their own debt while taxing you on dollars worth less every year.

23

Who loses?

- Anyone paid in wages.

- Anyone saving in cash.

- Anyone stuck in the system.

Inflation is the rich man's game. It transfers wealth *upward*—while you grind harder for shrinking dollars.

---

**Taxation: Legalized Theft Dressed as "Civic Duty"**

If inflation bleeds you slowly, taxes stab you openly.

The average person spends more on taxes than food, housing, and transportation—**combined.**

Here's how the game is rigged:

- **Earn a paycheck?** You're taxed first.

- **Spend what's left?** Sales tax.

- **Own a home?** Property tax.

- **Drive a car?** Registration and fuel taxes.

- **Die?** Estate tax.

You are taxed for living, earning, spending, saving, dying.

And the more you earn through *labor*, the more they take.

But the rich? They don't earn like you do.

They earn through:

- Capital gains

- Real estate depreciation

- Trusts and foundations

- Pass-through entities

These aren't loopholes. They're **exits**—and you were never shown the door.

The tax code isn't broken. It's a **code of rewards**—and it rewards those who play the owner's game, not the worker's game.

---

### Compound Theft: The Slow Drain You Never Feel

Here's the most brutal part of the financial prison: **you never feel the theft all at once.**

- A few percent inflation each year.

- A little more tax from that raise.

- A tiny bump in your cost of living.

- A slow erosion of savings that "just doesn't go as far anymore."

That's the genius of the system: **you never scream—because you never notice the bleeding.**

But over 10, 20, 30 years?

They've taken a fortune from you. Quietly. Systematically. Legally.

And you were told it was just "life."

---

Now you see it for what it is:

A system that pays you in dollars that die slowly, taxes you harder the more you grind, and steals silently while you think you're playing it safe.

But once you understand these weapons, you can stop being a victim—and start using **their game against them.**

# How Banks Profit While You Sink

Banks are not financial partners.
They're **financial predators** in suits.

You were taught to trust them. That putting your money in a savings account was "smart." That getting approved for a loan was an accomplishment. That a mortgage means stability.

Here's what you were never told:

**Banks make billions off your fear, your ignorance, and your blind trust.**

Let's break it down.

---

## 1. You Deposit, They Multiply

When you put $1,000 in a bank account, it doesn't sit there.

Thanks to **fractional reserve banking**, banks are allowed to keep just a *tiny fraction* of your deposit—and lend out the rest **up to 10x or more.**

That means:

- You deposit $1,000.

- The bank can legally create and loan out $9,000.

- They charge **interest** on money that **didn't exist** until you handed them your cash.

You get 0.01% interest on your savings (if that).
They collect 6%, 12%, 24%+ interest on loans they issued using *your* money.

That's not partnership. That's **legalized parasitism.**

---

## 2. Debt Is Their Primary Product

Banks don't sell financial freedom.
They sell **debt**—disguised as opportunity.

Credit cards. Mortgages. Auto loans. Personal loans. Student loans. All wrapped in marketing that makes you feel *grateful* to be approved.

But behind the scenes?

- They profit when you **carry a balance**.

- They profit when you **miss a payment**.

- They profit when you **refinance**.

- They profit when you **stay in debt longer**.

Their dream customer isn't rich. It's **perpetually broke, responsibly paying minimums forever.**

They don't want you to default. They don't want you to pay off everything either.
They want you in the **sweet spot of servitude.**

---

## 3. Mortgages = 30-Year Leashes

Buying a house with a mortgage is sold as "the American Dream." But for banks, it's the **ultimate income stream**.

A $300,000 loan at 6% interest over 30 years means you'll pay over **$350,000 in interest alone.** That's more than the house.

And who wins?

- The bank collects **interest upfront** (amortization schedules are rigged that way).

- They get a **house as collateral** (secured asset).

28

- If you miss payments, they **own your equity** and can foreclose.

You pay, they win.
Even in foreclosure, **they still win**—because they built the rules.

---

## 4. Fees, Fees, and More Fees

Banks rake in billions in so-called "service fees" every year:

- Overdraft fees

- ATM fees

- Maintenance fees

- Late payment fees

- Wire transfer fees

These aren't accidents. They're **engineered friction points**—designed to extract money from people who can least afford it.

And those same banks?

- Get bailed out by the government when they screw up.

- Offer near-zero interest while collecting double digits.

- Repackage debt, sell it on Wall Street, and profit *again*.

---

## Banks Don't Work for You—They Work for Themselves

They want your:

- **Deposits** (so they can lend)

- **Debt** (so they can collect)

- **Dependence** (so you never leave)

You think you're the customer.
But in reality, **you're the product.**

# Why 9-to-5 Keeps You Poor by Design

Wake up. Commute. Work. Commute. Crash. Repeat.

That's the cycle.

They call it "security."
They sell it as "purpose."
But behind the curtain, the 9-to-5 is nothing more than **a modern form of wage slavery.**

**It keeps you too tired to build, too taxed to grow, and too scared to leave.**

Let's break the illusion.

---

### 1. Time-for-Money Is a Broken Model

In a job, you trade time for a fixed paycheck.

It doesn't matter how hard you work, how much value you create, or how profitable the company becomes—you're still capped.

Meanwhile, the people above you—**owners, executives, shareholders**—get paid whether they work or not.

They have leverage.
You have a time clock.

This is why people stay stuck:

- You give 40+ hours a week.

- You pay 30–50% of your income in taxes.

- You get a 3% raise (if you're lucky).

- Inflation eats it before you even feel it.

31

Every dollar you earn is taxed *first*. Every hour you trade is gone *forever*.

But passive income? It keeps coming.
Business income? It scales.
Asset income? It multiplies.

Jobs don't give you those.
They give you just enough to keep you quiet.

---

## 2. The Psychological Trap

Jobs don't just drain your time.
They drain your **identity**.

You're trained to:

- Ask for permission to take a day off.

- Feel guilty for wanting more.

- Think rich people are "lucky" or "greedy."

You're made to feel like a *rebel* for asking, "What if I want freedom instead of just a paycheck?"

That's not an accident. It's programming.

Most people don't leave the 9-to-5 because they can't.
They stay because they've been mentally caged to believe **there's no alternative.**

---

## 3. Stability Is the Bait—Stagnation Is the Hook

Jobs feel safe. Predictable. Familiar.

But safety is a double-edged sword:

- It keeps you fed, but not full.

- It keeps you afloat, but never sailing.

- It keeps you dependent, and that's the point.

Because if you're dependent, you'll do as you're told. You'll tolerate low raises. You'll pay high taxes. You'll never question the system.

And even if you want out, you'll be too tired to act.

That's the strategy: **Exhaust the body. Numb the mind. Delay the dreams.**

---

**Here's the Final Truth:**

A job isn't freedom.
It's a leash with weekends off.

The rich don't work for income—they build **machines that print income.**
They don't trade time—they buy **leverage, ownership, and control.**

And that's what you're going to learn to build.

# Chapter 2 – Secrets of the 1%: The Money Rules They Never Teach You

## How the Elite Think Differently About Money

The real gap between the rich and everyone else?
It's not luck. It's not talent. It's not even education.

It's **thinking.** Specifically, how they think about **money, control, and power.**

You've been trained to think like a laborer.
They've been trained to think like a banker, a builder, a chess master.

And until you rewire your mindset, you'll keep playing a losing game—no matter how hard you hustle.

Let's flip the script.

---

**You Think Money Is Something You Earn.**

**They Think Money Is Something You Control.**

Most people trade hours for dollars.
The rich trade **assets, systems, and ideas** for cash flow.

You were taught to ask, "How much do I make?"
They ask, "What do I own that makes money for me?"

One is based on effort.
The other is based on **leverage.**

And that one mental shift changes everything.

---

## You See Money as a Goal.

## They See It as a Tool.

Most people dream of "having money."
The elite dream of what **they can do with it**—how they can **multiply**, **protect**, and **leverage** it.

That's why they don't hold cash—they move it.
They don't save—they **deploy**.
They don't fear risk—they **control** it through information, structure, and position.

The goal isn't to hoard money. The goal is to turn it into **power.**

---

## You Were Taught to Avoid Debt.

## They Use Debt to Build Empires.

You were told debt is dangerous.
The elite know: **bad debt traps you—good debt sets you free.**

- You borrow for consumption (cars, gadgets, vacations).

- They borrow for cash-flowing assets (real estate, businesses, investments).

You get interest bills.
They get tax deductions, appreciation, and monthly income.

And when done right?
**They don't even pay it back—their assets do.**

---

**You Try to Own Everything.**

**They Prefer to Control Everything.**

This is one of the most powerful—and most hidden—wealth philosophies:

**Own nothing. Control everything.**

Why?

Because ownership makes you a target. It exposes you to taxes, lawsuits, liabilities.
Control lets you benefit from assets **without having your name on them.**

How?

- Holding companies

- Trusts

- LLCs

- Foundations

While you're proudly putting your name on everything, they're quietly building **impenetrable wealth structures** no court or creditor can touch.

---

**You Were Taught to Be a Consumer.**

**They Think Like Capital Allocators.**

When the average person makes money, they spend it: new car, new clothes, upgraded lifestyle.

When the elite make money, they ask:
**"Where can this capital work the hardest for me?"**

They're not consumers.

They're **strategic investors, system builders, and opportunity hunters.**

---

### The Bottom Line

The 1% don't follow the rules you were taught—because **they were never meant to follow them. They were meant to write them.**

And now? So are you.

## Assets vs. Liabilities: What They *Really* Mean

Most people think they understand this.

They don't.

Ask the average person, "What's an asset?" and you'll hear:

- "My house."

- "My car."

- "My savings account."

Wrong. Wrong. And wrong.

Here's the brutal truth:

**If it doesn't put money in your pocket, it's not an asset. If it takes money out, it's a liability—no matter what the bankers or society tells you.**

Let's break this all the way down.

---

### The Lie: "Your Home Is Your Biggest Asset"

That's what they told you. That your house was your nest egg, your investment, your financial foundation.

Reality check:
If your house costs you money every month—**it's a liability.**

Mortgage, taxes, maintenance, insurance, upgrades—it all drains cash flow.

Now, can a house appreciate over time? Sure.

But here's the 1% play:

- They buy **income-producing property** (rental real estate).

38

- The tenant covers all expenses.

- The property appreciates over time.

- They write off depreciation.

- They refinance to pull out tax-free money.

- They 1031 exchange to avoid taxes and level up again.

That's an **asset.**
Your primary residence? Emotionally fulfilling—financially draining.

---

### The Truth: Assets Pay You—Liabilities Cost You

Here's how to think like the wealthy:

**An asset = anything that generates income or appreciates while producing cash flow.**
**A liability = anything that requires you to feed it.**

Let's compare:

| Item | Cash Flow? | Appreciates? | Asset or Liability? |
|---|---|---|---|
| Rental Property | ✔ | ✔ | Asset |
| Your Home | ✘ | Maybe | Liability (for now) |
| Stock Dividend Portfolio | ✔ | ✔ | Asset |
| New Car (Financed) | ✘ | ✘ | Liability |
| iPhone 15 Pro Max | ✘ | ✘ | Liability |
| Vending Machine Route | ✔ | N/A | Asset |
| Business You Own | ✔ | ✔ | Asset |

This is how the 1% evaluate every purchase:
**Will this make me richer, or poorer?**
**Will this feed me, or will I have to feed it?**

---

### Liabilities Are Fine—If You Use Assets to Pay for Them

Here's where the elite truly separate from the masses:

They don't deny themselves nice things.
They just make sure **assets pay for them.**

- Want the Lambo? Buy real estate that covers the monthly lease.

- Want the Rolex? Use cash flow from an ecommerce store.

- Want a luxury trip? Let your stock dividends pay the bill.

**Assets first. Flex later.**

The broke mindset buys liabilities with labor.
The rich mindset buys assets with strategy—and lets those assets fund the lifestyle.

# The "Control Everything, Own Nothing" Philosophy

This idea is so foreign to the average person, it sounds backwards.

You were taught to *own* things:

- Own your house.

- Own your car.

- Own your business.

But the ultra-rich? They follow a different rule:

**Own nothing. Control everything.**

Because **ownership makes you a target.**
Control makes you powerful—and **invisible.**

Let me explain.

---

### Ownership Is Exposure

When something is legally in your name, it's vulnerable to:

- Lawsuits

- Divorce

- Creditors

- Taxes

- Government scrutiny

If you own 10 rental properties in your name, a single lawsuit could jeopardize **everything.**

If you own a successful business in your personal name, you're exposed.

If you die, the government might come after your estate for **40%+** in taxes. That's the cost of ownership… when you're unprotected.

---

**Control Is Protection**

Now let's flip the script.

What if those properties weren't owned by *you*, but by **LLCs**?

What if your business was owned by a **holding company**?

What if your personal wealth was tucked inside **trusts, foundations, or offshore entities**—and you simply controlled them?

Now your name's not on anything.
But you still call the shots.
Still collect the income.
Still live with full access and benefit—**but no exposure.**

That's not fraud. That's **strategy.**
Used legally. By the wealthy. Every single day.

---

**Real-World Examples:**

- **Your House**: Owned by a trust. You live in it. Legally, it's not "yours."

- **Your Business**: Owned by a holding company. You control it as a manager or officer.

- **Your Vehicles**: Owned by your company. Tax-deductible, protected.

- **Your Investments**: Held in an LLC or trust. You direct the moves, but creditors can't touch them.

This is how dynasties are built.
The paper trail ends before it reaches them.
Lawsuits hit walls. Taxes find nothing.

Because they don't *own* the chessboard.
They just move the pieces.

---

### This Is the Game You Were Never Taught

They told you to build assets in your name.

But when you do that:

- You become the legal owner = full exposure.

- You take on the liability.

- You get taxed harder.

The wealthy build **layers. Structures. Shields.**
Not because they're paranoid—but because **they understand power.**

# The Elite's Financial Structures — Explained & Compared

This isn't theory. These are the **actual weapons** the 1% deploy daily to **protect, grow,** and **control** their wealth—**while staying invisible and untouchable.**

You were never told about these tools because they weren't built for you.
They were built to protect **them from you.**

But now?
**You're about to steal the blueprint.**

You don't win the money game by playing harder. You win by **playing smarter,** with the right legal vehicles carrying your wealth.

Here's how the rich use **LLCs, Trusts, Private Foundations, and Private Banking Systems**—what they are, how they work, and how you can use them.

---

## LLC – *Limited Liability Company*

**Want to build cash flow and protection into your business or investments? This is step one.**

An **LLC (Limited Liability Company)** is the foundation. It creates a legal wall between *you* and *your assets*. If something goes wrong, the liability stops at the company—not your house, not your car, not your savings.

**Purpose:**
To operate businesses, hold assets, or conduct income-generating activities **without personal liability.**

**What it does:**

- Protects your personal assets from lawsuits related to the business.

- Allows tax flexibility (pass-through taxation or S-Corp election).

- Provides privacy (in certain states).

- Enables you to deduct business expenses legally.

**How the rich use it:**

- Each real estate property = its own LLC, limiting legal exposure.

- Operating companies are placed **under holding company LLCs** for control and insulation.

- Often layered with trusts for ultimate protection.

---

**Trust –** *Asset Protection + Estate Control Tool*

**What it is:**
A legal agreement where one party (the **trustee**) holds and manages assets for the benefit of another (the **beneficiary**), under specific terms. A **trust** is a legal container that holds your assets. But here's the trick: **you don't own them anymore. The trust does.**

**Types of Trusts:**

- **Revocable Living Trust** (can be changed, avoids probate)

- **Irrevocable Trust** (cannot be changed, but offers superior protection)

- **Dynasty Trust** (multi-generational wealth transfer with tax protection)

**What it does:**

- Removes assets from your personal estate.

- Protects assets from lawsuits, creditors, and estate taxes.

- Keeps your wealth **off public record.**

- Ensures generational control (e.g., kids don't blow the inheritance).

**How the rich use it:**

- Their name isn't on the mansion, yacht, or business—the **trust** owns it.

- Their will? It's in the trust—no probate court, no taxes, no drama.

- They stay "broke" on paper—but control millions.

---

**Private Foundation – *Control + Tax Weapon***

**What it is:**
A tax-exempt entity set up to manage charitable giving—**controlled by you or your family.**

**Want to move millions tax-free, fund your legacy, and still control the cash? That's what a private foundation is for.**

The public thinks foundations are for "giving back."
But the wealthy know better: foundations are **control vehicles.**

**What it does:**

- Lets you **donate assets** to the foundation (and get a deduction).

- You still **control how the money is used** (salaries, grants, initiatives).

- Avoids capital gains tax on appreciated assets.

- Can fund projects that align with your values *and* benefit your legacy.

**How the rich use it:**

- Move money out of their estate—**tax-free**.

- Pay family members a salary to "run" the foundation.

- Create legacy influence while keeping the money **in their ecosystem**.

It's charity on the outside. Control on the inside.

---

### Private Banking / Infinite Banking Concept – *Becoming the Bank*

**What it is:**
A high-cash-value **whole life insurance policy** structured for maximum savings and **minimal death benefit.**

**Want to borrow money without credit checks, taxes, or begging banks for approval? The rich don't borrow from banks. They borrow from themselves.**

This is the **Infinite Banking Concept**—a wealth strategy using high-cash-value **whole life insurance.**

**What it does:**

- Builds cash value that grows **tax-deferred**.

- Lets you borrow against that value **tax-free**.

- Keeps growing even when you borrow from it (non-direct recognition).

- Offers asset protection in most states.

**How the rich use it:**

- Store liquidity outside of banks.

- Borrow from themselves to invest in real estate, businesses, etc.

- Avoid taxes and bypass the banking system.

- Use it as a **private vault + tax-free lending system.**

Think of it as a **legal money multiplier** wrapped in an insurance policy.

---

**Quick Comparison Table:**

| Tool | Primary Use | Tax Benefit? | Asset Protection? | Control? | Used By the Rich For... |
|------|-------------|--------------|-------------------|----------|-------------------------|
| **LLC** | Business & asset holding | Yes | Yes | High | Running companie owning real estate |
| **Trust** | Estate planning & privacy | Yes | Very high | High (if trustee) | Wealth transfer, lawsuit shielding |
| **Private Foundation** | Charitable control | Huge | Moderate | Very high | Avoiding estate taxes, legacy influence |
| **Private Banking** | Asset growth & borrowing | Yes | High | Very high | Storing cash, tax-free loans |

---

**The Rich Don't Use One Tool—They Stack Them**

Example:

- **LLCs** hold each rental property.

- Those LLCs are owned by a **Holding Company**.

- That Holding Company is owned by a **Trust**.

- The cash flow is parked in a **Private Bank Policy**.

- Legacy and charity are handled by a **Private Foundation**.

On paper? They're broke.
In reality? They control millions. And no one can touch it.

# Chapter 3 – Wealth Myths That Keep You Broke

## Myth: Save Your Way to Wealth

You've heard it your whole life:
"Just save 10% of your income."
"Cut back on coffee."
"Live below your means."
"Be disciplined, and one day… you'll be rich."

**That's a lie. A seductive one. A deadly one.**

Here's the truth:

**You cannot save your way to financial freedom.**
Not in this economy. Not in this system. Not with these rules.

Let's break this down—fast and hard.

---

### The Numbers Don't Work

Let's say you make $60,000/year. You manage to save 10% ($6,000).
You do this for 30 years. Let's be generous and say you earn 5% annually on that money.

That gives you around **$400,000** before taxes and inflation.

Sounds decent?

Now subtract:

- 30 years of inflation eating the value.

- Taxes when you pull it out (yes, your 401(k) gets taxed).

- Emergencies, life expenses, market corrections.

What you're left with isn't wealth. It's **a cushion. Maybe.**

Meanwhile, in those same 30 years:

- Inflation eroded the dollar.

- Housing and healthcare costs exploded.

- The rich doubled their net worth *every few years* using **leverage and assets.**

Saving is **defensive.**
Wealth-building is **offensive.**

---

### The System Punishes Savers

Banks want your money—not to protect it, but to **use it against you.**

You save $10,000? They lend out $100,000.
You get 0.01% interest. They charge borrowers 7%, 15%, 25%.

You're playing *checkers* in a **chess game built by thieves.**

And while you sit on your savings like a responsible adult, three enemies are quietly destroying your money:

1. **Inflation** – You lose purchasing power every year.

2. **Taxes** – Interest you earn is taxed (even if it's pennies).

3. **Opportunity Cost** – That same money could've been working harder **elsewhere.**

**The savers get slaughtered. The deployers get rich.**

---

**What the Rich Do Instead**

The 1% don't save. They **store and deploy.**

Here's what that looks like:

- They park money in **cash-flowing assets**, not bank accounts.

- They use **insurance policies** and **trusts** to store value *tax-free.*

- They keep liquidity in **private banks,** where it earns and can be borrowed against.

- They leverage capital into **income streams**, not rainy-day funds.

If they do keep savings, it's only for **quick-strike investments**, not "security."

Security is a myth. **Cash flow is king.**

---

**So What Do You Do Instead?**

- **Stop saving for safety. Start storing for leverage.**

- **Stop thinking "How can I save more?" Start asking "Where can I deploy this for cash flow?"**

- Build a war chest—not a piggy bank.

- Use vehicles like:

    o   Business ownership

    o   Rental real estate

    o   Dividend-paying stocks

    o   Digital income streams

- o   Infinite banking policies

And always remember:

**Saving is what they told the middle class to do… while the rich were buying the world.**

# Myth: Get a Safe Job, Retire Rich

This is the lie that built the cubicle farm.
That created the 40-year career grind.
That sold millions on the illusion of security in exchange for **life energy.**

"Get a safe job."
"Stick with it."
"Climb the ladder."
"Retire comfortably."

But look around.

**The people who followed this advice the closest are now broke, burned out, or barely hanging on.**

Let's dismantle this toxic fairy tale.

---

### The "Safe Job" Doesn't Exist Anymore

Corporations don't care about loyalty.
They don't care how long you've been there.
They don't care how hard you work.

- Pensions? Gone.

- Lifetime employment? Gone.

- Healthcare coverage? Shrinking.

- Cost of living raises? A joke.

You are an expense. If the bottom line drops or AI replaces your function, you're out—**with nothing to show but a resume.**

This isn't fear-mongering. It's **reality.**

Millions have learned the hard way:

**There is nothing safe about depending on one source of income you don't control.**

---

### Retirement? That Was Never for You

The entire concept of retirement was built for a different world:

- One-income households
- Low inflation
- Solid pensions
- Shorter lifespans

Today?

- You'll live longer.
- Your dollar buys less.
- Your investments are taxed.
- And most retirement accounts are glorified **delayed tax bombs.**

Think about it:

- You work 40+ years.
- Save in a 401(k) you don't control.
- Hope the market doesn't crash before you retire.
- Withdraw the money—and get **taxed like a sucker.**

That's not wealth. That's **a slow-motion trap.**

---

### The Corporate Ladder Is a Lie

Even if you climb the ladder, what's at the top?

- More hours

- More pressure

- Higher taxes

- Less time

- And if you die early? The system keeps your contributions.

Compare that to owning a business, equity, or income-producing assets that:

- Work without your presence

- Scale without your time

- Can be passed to your children

- Can't be "laid off"

**That's real security.**

---

### The 1% Don't Work Jobs—They *Buy* Them

They:

- Buy businesses, not clock into them.

- Hire teams, not join them.

- Acquire systems that print income—**while you check your PTO balance.**

Jobs are a temporary tool, not a long-term wealth strategy.

**If your income stops when you stop working, you don't own freedom—you rent it.**

**The Truth**

A "safe job" is the slowest, most expensive way to live a mediocre life.
Retirement is not an end goal—it's a system shutdown.

Your real power comes from:

- Building assets now

- Creating cash flow now

- Taking control now

The job was never the plan. It was the **distraction from the plan.**

# Myth: Buy a House—It's an Investment

You've been told your whole life:

- "Renting is throwing money away."

- "Your home is your biggest asset."

- "Real estate always goes up."

- "Owning a home is the American Dream."

Let's translate that:

**"Please tie yourself to a 30-year loan, take on all the risk, and call it success."**

Because behind the fantasy of ownership is one cold reality:

**Your house isn't an investment. It's a liability.**

---

### Let's Define It: What's an Investment?

An investment:

- **Produces income**

- **Appreciates in value**

- **Can be leveraged**

- **Gives you liquidity or cash flow**

Now ask yourself:

- Does your house pay you every month?

- Can you sell it quickly, without friction or cost?

- Does it increase your monthly income?

- Can you write off the expenses or depreciation?

58

**No. No. No. And mostly, no.**

Then it's not an investment. It's **a lifestyle expense with a mortgage.**

---

### Here's the Truth:

- You pay the mortgage, the taxes, the insurance, the repairs.
- You can't write off depreciation like a rental property.
- You're on the hook when the roof leaks, the AC dies, or the neighborhood declines.
- It doesn't pay you. **You feed it.**

And unless you're house-hacking or renting out rooms, it does **nothing to move you toward freedom.**

---

### The Appreciation Lie

"But my house is worth more than when I bought it!"

Sure. But so is:

- Gas
- Groceries
- Healthcare
- Everything else—**because of inflation**

If you bought a house for $300K and sold it 10 years later for $400K:

- Subtract interest paid
- Subtract closing costs

- Subtract realtor fees

- Subtract taxes

- Subtract maintenance and upgrades

You might have made *some* money—**but was it wealth-building, cash-flowing income?**

Or just *delayed equity* wrapped in decades of expense?

---

### Who Really Wins?

Follow the money:

- **Banks** get decades of interest.

- **The government** gets property tax forever.

- **Insurance companies** collect premiums.

- **Contractors and realtors** get paid every time you make a move.

You provide the capital, the labor, and the liability.
They collect the profits.

That's not an investment. That's **a transfer of wealth disguised as tradition.**

---

### What the Rich Do Instead

The wealthy:

- Rent where they live if it's cheaper or gives them flexibility.

- Buy **income-producing** properties (rentals, multifamily, Airbnb).

- Write off depreciation, travel to check on properties, refinance tax-free.

- Control equity and cash flow without *ever* calling a plumber themselves.

They know the goal isn't to "own a house."
It's to **own cash-flowing real estate—without living in it.**

---

### You Want a Home? Fine. But Know the Game.

Buy one because you love it.
Because you want control.
Because it's where your family feels stable.

But don't fool yourself.

**It's not an investment. It's a personal purchase with massive costs.**

The true investment is something that pays you, not something you pay for until you're 60.

# Myth: If You Work Hard, You'll Win

This is the most dangerous lie ever sold.
Not because it's false—
But because it's **half true.**

Hard work **does matter. But it's not enough.**
Not even close.

The system wants you to believe that effort equals reward.
So you'll keep grinding, sacrificing, and obeying—**without ever questioning why you're not winning.**

But here's the harsh reality:

**Hard work doesn't make you rich.**
**Leverage does.**

---

### Look Around—Who's Winning?

The people doing backbreaking labor?

- Construction workers

- Nurses

- Delivery drivers

- Warehouse staff

- Teachers

They work their asses off—and they're barely making it.

Meanwhile, the ones at the top?

- Run systems

- Own assets

- Make moves with capital, not sweat

- Work less but **earn more**

They don't work harder than you.
They **work smarter with positioning, scale, and control.**

---

## Why the System Loves This Lie

Because if you believe hard work is the key, you'll:

- Stay loyal to jobs that don't serve you

- Judge others for "getting rich too fast"

- Feel guilty for wanting more

- Sacrifice time, health, and family without ever questioning the game

They need you to believe this so you'll **keep powering the machine**.

**If everyone realized leverage beats labor, the system would collapse.**

---

## Hard Work Without Leverage = Slavery

Let's define this clearly:

- **Hard Work = Input**

- **Leverage = Output Multiplier**

Leverage is what turns one hour of effort into 100 hours of results:

- Media that scales (books, videos, courses)

- Businesses with employees or automation

- Real estate that pays you monthly

- Money that earns while you sleep

- Code, content, systems, deals

**Leverage = exponential return.**
Hard work without it = **exhaustion with no exit.**

---

## The 1% Use Work Differently

They work hard—but only *on the right things:*

- Building assets

- Acquiring leverage

- Structuring deals

- Positioning capital

They don't grind endlessly. They **build once, and get paid forever.**

That's the real game.

And until you stop selling your time and start multiplying your impact—you're not even on the board.

---

## Final Word on the Myth

Working hard makes you **valuable—**
But only to someone else.

Want freedom?
Work **strategically.** Work on **scalable assets.** Work toward **ownership.**

That's how you win.

# Chapter 4 – Secret Loopholes of the Rich

## The Real Tax Game (And How You're Playing It Wrong)

You were taught taxes are just a part of life.
That if you make more, you pay more.
That it's patriotic, fair, and unavoidable.

**That's a lie.**

**The rich don't pay taxes like you. They don't play by the same rules. And they never will.**

Because the tax code isn't a punishment—it's a **blueprint.**
A rulebook written **by the rich, for the rich**, to incentivize exactly what they do.

And here's the sick part: it's not hidden.
It's right in front of you—you just weren't taught how to read it.

---

### W-2 Income: The Highest-Taxed Game on the Board

Let's start with the worst way to make money: a job.

- You earn a salary.

- Taxes come out *before* you see a dime.

- You're taxed on your **gross** income.

- Then you pay state taxes, sales tax, property tax, capital gains tax if you invest…

By the time you use your money, **you've been drained.**

Now compare that to how the rich make money:

- Through businesses, assets, and capital gains.

- They're taxed **last**, not first.

- They can defer, deduct, depreciate, and redirect.

- And many times? **They pay nothing. Legally.**

---

### The Tax Code Rewards Owners, Not Workers

Here's the dirty truth:

**The IRS gives tax breaks to people who do what the government wants: create jobs, provide housing, invest in the economy.**

Who does that?

- **Business owners**

- **Real estate investors**

- **Asset holders**

- **Capital allocators**

You were told to be a good worker.
They were taught to become **economic engines**—and get rewarded for it.

---

**Key Tax Loopholes the Rich Use (That You're Not)**

Let's break down the actual weapons:

**1. Business Deductions**

Run a business? You can write off:

- Your car

- Your phone

- Your laptop

- Travel

- Meals

- Part of your home

- Your health insurance

**You spend money anyway. The rich just do it through an entity—so it becomes deductible.**

You spend $1,000 and lose it.
They spend $1,000 and **write it off.**

**2. Real Estate Depreciation**

Own rental property? The IRS lets you **deduct the "loss in value"** over time—even if the value is going up.

This lets you:

- Earn cash flow

- Pay no tax on it

- Keep more money

- Roll it into more assets

They even use **cost segregation** to accelerate depreciation and create paper losses they can use against other income.

### 3. 1031 Exchanges

Sell a property? Normally you pay capital gains.
But with a 1031 exchange, you can **roll the profits into another property—tax-free.**

You can keep doing this indefinitely, growing your portfolio without ever paying the IRS.

### 4. Pay Yourself Through a Corporation

Instead of earning as a W-2 employee, the rich:

- Pay themselves through **S-Corps or LLCs**

- Take lower salaries, higher distributions (lower tax)

- Use **retirement plans** to shelter income

- Deduct business expenses before paying themselves

You get taxed on what you make.
They get taxed on **what's left after they play the game.**

---

### The Endgame: Eliminate Taxes *Legally*

At the highest levels, the rich:

- Borrow against appreciating assets (real estate, stocks, policies)

- Live off **tax-free loans**

- Use trusts and foundations to shift income

- Pass down wealth **without triggering estate taxes**

Their goal isn't to *pay less* tax.
Their goal is to **pay none**—by never triggering taxable events in the first place.

---

### You're Playing Defense. They're Playing Chess.

You file in April and hope for a refund.
They plan their entire year around tax *positioning*.

You avoid the IRS out of fear.
They leverage the code with confidence.

You follow the system.
They **own the rulebook.**

# How to Use Debt to Build Wealth

You were taught to fear debt.
Avoid credit cards. Pay off loans fast. Stay "debt-free."

And while you were cutting up cards and celebrating paying off your car...

**The rich were using debt to buy assets, scale empires, and pay zero taxes—without spending their own money.**

Debt isn't evil. Debt is **a weapon.**
The only question is: are you being hunted by it, or are you wielding it?

---

## The Two Types of Debt (One Destroys You, One Makes You Rich)

Let's define the difference:

### ✖ Bad Debt

- Spent on liabilities (cars, clothes, vacations)

- Costs you money monthly

- Depreciates instantly

- No cash flow, no return

Bad debt **enslaves.**

### ✅ Good Debt

- Used to acquire income-producing assets

- Paid back by renters, customers, or profits

- Can be deducted on taxes

- Leverages other people's money for your gain

Good debt **scales.**

The average person borrows to consume.
The rich borrow to control and cash-flow.

---

### How the Rich Use Debt Like a Weapon

### Real Estate Leverage

They put 20% down (sometimes less), borrow 80%, and let **tenants** pay off the loan.

- Rent covers the mortgage

- Property appreciates

- They deduct interest and depreciation

- They refinance, pull out equity **tax-free**, and repeat

They never "pay off the house"—because that would **kill the leverage.**

### Business Credit

The rich build **business credit** under LLCs and corporations, separate from their personal name.

They use it to:

- Finance marketing campaigns

- Purchase inventory

- Scale systems

- Float cash flow

And if they know the game? They **stack** business credit cards with 0% interest for 12–18 months, turning debt into **free expansion fuel.**

**Asset-Backed Lending**

Instead of selling stocks or property (which triggers taxes), the wealthy **borrow against them**.

- They use margin loans

- HELOCs (Home Equity Lines of Credit)

- Loans against whole life insurance cash value (infinite banking)

- Asset-backed lines from private banks

They're liquid. They're free to move. And the best part?

**Loans aren't income. They aren't taxed. Ever.**

That's the cheat code.

---

**You're Playing the Wrong Game**

You're told to:

- Save for 10 years

- Then buy something

- Then slowly pay it off

The wealthy?

- Borrow now

- Acquire the asset

- Let the asset pay the loan

72

- Keep scaling

You're "playing it safe" while they're building kingdoms with **other people's money.**

---

**But Isn't Debt Risky?**

Yes—**if you're using it like a consumer.**

But when you:

- Use debt for **cash-flowing assets**

- Have a plan to exit or roll it forward

- Maintain liquidity and insurance

- Protect with legal structures

Then it becomes **controlled firepower.**

The middle class fears debt.
The wealthy master it—and ride it to freedom.

# Legal Protections and Income Hiding

The more you make, the bigger the target on your back.

Lawsuits. Creditors. Divorce. Taxes. Government overreach.
One slip, and everything you've built can be **stripped overnight—unless you protect it first.**

That's why the 1% don't just build wealth…

**They armor it. Shield it. Hide it.**

And they do it **legally**—through smart structures and airtight strategy.

---

### Why You Need Legal Armor

Ask yourself:

- Do you have anything in your name?

- Could someone sue you and take it?

- Could the IRS see your full income stream?

- Could a divorce destroy your empire?

If the answer is "yes," you're playing the **most dangerous game—** wealth without protection.

The rich never play like that.

They know the truth:

**Privacy is power. Ownership is risk. Visibility is vulnerability.**

So here's how they stay off the radar and untouchable.

---

## 1. Anonymous LLCs

Certain U.S. states (like Wyoming, Delaware, New Mexico) allow you to create **LLCs with full privacy.**

- Your name never appears publicly.

- You can own real estate, vehicles, IP, or other businesses through the LLC.

- Lawsuits hit the entity—not you.

- The paper trail stops cold.

**You control the assets—but don't technically "own" them.**

---

## 2. Irrevocable Trusts

The ultimate legal firewall.

- Move your wealth into a trust.

- You no longer legally own it.

- But you can still control distribution, timing, and beneficiaries.

**Creditors can't touch it. Ex-spouses can't seize it. The IRS can't easily assess it.**

Used with offshore variations? It becomes nearly **bulletproof.**

---

## 3. Private Foundations

We covered these before—but here's the stealth power move:

- Shift appreciated assets into a foundation.

- Avoid capital gains tax.

- Retain control over spending.

- Fund salaries, operations, and family "projects" under a nonprofit umbrella.

It's not tax evasion. It's **tax optimization through legacy building.**

---

### 4. Private Contracts & Income Structuring

The rich often don't receive income through W-2 or obvious bank transfers.

They use:

- **Management fees**

- **Licensing agreements**

- **Royalty structures**

- **Asset leasing**

- **Offshore accounts and deferred comp plans**

Example:
A real estate investor has their **LLC pay a consulting fee** to another entity they own in a no-tax state. That entity then **leases a car, pays for travel**, and **funnels the rest into a trust.**

On paper? Their income is minimal.
In practice? They're living at a **private-jet level.**

---

### 5. Income Obfuscation: Keeping Eyes Off the Money

The goal isn't to lie. The goal is to **structure.**

The wealthy don't hide income illegally.
They **redirect it through legal means** that:

- Delay taxation

- Lower audit risk

- Minimize public visibility

- Shield from civil lawsuits

They don't brag about wealth. They **bury it under layers of control.**

---

**Bottom Line: Be the Ghost With the Machine**

- Own nothing. Control everything.

- Stay lean on paper, but powerful in reality.

- Use entities as armor. Use contracts as swords.

- Don't play flashy. Play **fortified.**

Wealth without protection is a ticking time bomb.
Wealth with protection is **dynasty-level power.**

# Infinite Banking: Turning Yourself Into Your Own Bank

You were taught to keep your money in a bank.
The rich? They **become** the bank.

And they do it using a tool that sounds boring—but is secretly one of the most powerful wealth engines ever built:

**High-Cash-Value Whole Life Insurance**
(Engineered specifically for Infinite Banking)

This isn't your grandma's policy.
This is a **private banking system** disguised as life insurance—used to **store, grow, and deploy capital** in a way that's untouchable by the IRS, the banks, or market crashes.

---

### What Is Infinite Banking?

Infinite Banking is a strategy where you:

1. Set up a high-cash-value whole life policy with a **mutual insurance company**

2. **Overfund** it—meaning most of your premium goes to **cash value**, not death benefit

3. Let that cash value **grow tax-deferred**, with guaranteed interest + dividends

4. Borrow against that value—**tax-free, anytime, no questions asked**

5. Pay it back if and when you want—or **not at all**

Your money keeps growing inside the policy, even while you borrow against it.
That's the key. You don't withdraw—you **leverage.**

**Why the Rich Love It**

- **Tax-free compounding** of capital

- **Tax-free borrowing** of large amounts of money

- **No credit checks, no banks, no gatekeepers**

- **Lawsuit-proof in most states**

- **No 1099s, no IRS reporting**

- **Guaranteed returns + annual dividends**

Let's say you have $200,000 in cash value.
You borrow $100,000 to buy real estate or fund a deal.
Your $200K **still grows in full**—as if it was never touched.

Try doing that with a savings account.

**What Happens If You Don't Repay the Loan?**

That's where this gets even more powerful.

- You're not withdrawing your money—you're **borrowing against it.**

- The policy loan is secured by your **death benefit.**

- If you die with an outstanding balance, it's simply deducted from what your heirs receive.

**No penalties. No taxes. No collections.**

Your collateral is built-in. Your repayment schedule is **optional.**

That's why many high-net-worth families:

- Borrow millions over their lifetime

- Never repay the loans

- Use the policy as a **tax-free vault**

- Leave the remainder to heirs—**still tax-free**

---

## What Can You Use Policy Loans For?

Anything.

- Real estate investments

- Business capital

- Paying off bad debt

- Private deals

- Funding your lifestyle

- Buying other insurance or income-producing assets

There are **no restrictions**—because you're borrowing from your own private banking system.

---

## How to Actually Get This Kind of Insurance (The Right Way)

**Important:** Not all insurance agents understand Infinite Banking. To avoid getting the wrong policy, **look for an IBC-certified advisor** (via the Nelson Nash Institute) or a proven **wealth strategist** who specializes in high-cash-value policy design. Avoid traditional agents who focus on death benefit over cash value—they'll sell you the wrong product.

Not all whole life insurance policies are created equal.
You don't want what the average insurance agent tries to sell.

You need a policy **specifically designed** for Infinite Banking.

✅ **What Kind of Policy You Need:**

- **Whole life insurance** (not term, not universal)

- **From a mutual insurance company** (so you receive dividends)

- **Structured for maximum cash value**, not death benefit

- Includes a **Paid-Up Additions (PUA) rider** to supercharge early liquidity

❌ **Red Flags to Avoid:**

- High commissions / low cash value in early years

- Indexed or variable policies (tied to the stock market = volatile)

- Agents who don't understand Infinite Banking—**you need a specialist**

**How to Set It Up:**

1. **Work with an Infinite Banking practitioner** (not a standard life insurance agent)

2. Decide how much you want to contribute monthly/yearly

3. Have the policy designed for **high liquidity and low fees**

4. Review **illustrations** showing cash value, loan potential, and growth year-by-year

5. Fund the policy and **access capital on your terms**

**Trusted Companies Often Used:**

- MassMutual

- Guardian Life

- Penn Mutual

- Lafayette Life

- New York Life

These are **mutual companies** with strong dividend history and policy flexibility.

---

## How Fast Can You Use the Money?

Usually within **30–60 days** of funding.

A well-structured policy can give you **60%–90% liquidity in Year 1**.
This means if you put in $50,000, you might have **$40,000+** available to use **right away.**

And remember:
Your full amount continues growing—even while you borrow against it.

---

## Why Infinite Banking Works:

You're not just buying insurance. You're building a **financial vault** that gives you:

- Control

- Privacy

- Liquidity

- Predictable growth

- Tax-free deployment

- Protection from lawsuits and banks

The middle class begs for loans.
The rich **loan money to themselves**.

And now? So will you.

# Chapter 5 – Hidden Financial Moves You Were Never Meant to See

## Arbitrage: Geographic, Labor, and Currency

Most people try to get rich by **earning more.**

The wealthy? They get rich by **exploiting value gaps.**

That's arbitrage:

**The art of profiting from price or value differences between two places, markets, or systems.**

Arbitrage isn't risky.
It's **predictable**—if you know what to look for.

And the truth is, you've been living inside a bubble that's **overpriced, overtaxed, and overhyped**—while real opportunities lie just outside your borders.

---

### 1. Geographic Arbitrage

This is when you **earn in a strong currency or economy**—but **live or spend in a cheaper one.**

It's the reason:

- Digital nomads live like kings in Bali or Thailand on $3,000/month.

- Entrepreneurs leave California for Texas or Florida.

- Millionaires move their HQs to Puerto Rico (for the **4% tax rate** under Act 60).

**The Play:**

- Make USD, spend in pesos, baht, or rupiah.

- Live in low-cost, high-luxury zones (SE Asia, Eastern Europe, Latin America).

- Cut your burn rate by 50–70% while maintaining income.

If your online business earns $10K/month, you're middle class in NYC…
But **wealthy** in Lisbon, Medellín, or Tbilisi.

**It's not about being cheap. It's about buying power.**

---

**2. Labor Arbitrage**

This is how empires are scaled:

**Hire in one country, sell in another.**

The rich:

- Hire $5/hour virtual assistants in the Philippines.

- Use $15/hour coders in Eastern Europe.

- Build agencies with global teams at a fraction of local payroll.

Meanwhile, clients in the U.S., U.K., or Australia are paying **premium rates**—and never see the labor delta.

You're not exploiting people—you're **leveraging economics.**

It's the exact play Amazon, Apple, and every Fortune 500 company runs:
**Low-cost labor, high-margin output.**

You can do it too—at any scale.

---

### Currency Arbitrage (The Elite's Quiet Power Play)

You've heard of people making money trading forex. Fast charts, fast money, fast losses.

But that's not how the rich play the game.

**Real currency arbitrage isn't trading—it's positioning.**
It's how the wealthy store value, dodge inflation, and play offense with strong currencies and weak economies.

And it's a long game.

---

### What Currency Arbitrage Really Means

It's not day-trading. It's not gambling.
It's the art of:

- **Holding stronger currencies** when your local one weakens

- **Buying assets** in depressed currency zones

- **Exchanging value** between systems others don't understand

The goal isn't to flip for fast profit.
It's to **safeguard purchasing power**, move like a sovereign, and find **asymmetrical plays** in global markets.

---

**How the Wealthy Actually Use Currency Arbitrage:**

**1. Multi-Currency Holding Accounts**

They hold USD, EUR, CHF, SGD, or gold-backed digital currencies through:

- Private banking institutions

- Family offices

- Offshore corporate accounts

For readers starting out, entry-level tools like **Wise** or **Revolut** can simulate this approach, helping you manage money across borders. **They're not elite tools—but they're gateways.**

Use them to:

- Pay international contractors

- Convert and hold small amounts across major currencies

- Gain awareness of currency strength over time

**2. Store Value Outside Weakening Economies**

If your country's fiat is unstable, inflationary, or volatile:

- Move capital into stronger, more stable currencies

- Protect your purchasing power when your home currency drops

This isn't profit-seeking—it's **financial defense**.

**3. Buy Assets in Currency-Collapsing Regions**

Here's where the play gets real—but advanced:

Let's say:

- The Colombian peso drops 30% against the dollar.

- Real estate in Medellín becomes dirt cheap in USD terms.

- You buy property or land while the local economy bottoms out.

- Over time, the **property appreciates** and the **currency rebounds**.

That's **double upside**.

But this isn't for beginners. It requires:

- Legal guidance

- Local market knowledge

- Boots-on-the-ground contacts

- Real liquidity

**Most readers won't start here—but they need to understand that these doors exist.** The rich walk through them while everyone else stays stuck.

### 4. Crypto-Fiat Arbitrage (Advanced, Frontier Play)

In countries with capital controls or cash shortages:

- Crypto can trade at a **premium or discount** to fiat

- You can buy stablecoins (USDT, USDC)

- You can bridge currencies across borders **without a bank**

This requires deep knowledge of:

- Local crypto laws

- Platform liquidity

- On/off-ramp restrictions

But used correctly, it's **next-level sovereignty**.

**The Reality Check**

**This is not a get-rich tactic. It's a strategic lens.**

Currency arbitrage requires:

- Patience

- Research

- Capital

- Legal awareness

- Cultural intelligence

For most readers, this chapter is not a call to action—it's a **shift in worldview.**
A reminder that money moves across borders, and those who understand the movement **win quietly and consistently.**

**Start Here:**

- Open a multi-currency account (Revolut, Wise) just to watch flows

- Track currency strength vs. your native fiat

- Study how the wealthy preserve value globally

- Get curious—not reckless

Currency arbitrage isn't about making fast moves.
It's about making **unseen moves** that preserve and multiply wealth across borders.

# Business Credit Stacking and Leveraged Income

If you're still bootstrapping everything with your personal savings, you're playing the game in **slow motion**.

The wealthy don't scale businesses with their own money.
They don't risk personal credit.
They **build business credit**, stack multiple lines, and **borrow at 0% interest** to create income-generating machines—then repeat.

Let's break it all the way down.

---

### What Is Business Credit Stacking?

**Business credit stacking** is a strategy where you apply for multiple **high-limit business credit cards or lines of credit** in a short time frame—before those accounts appear on your credit file.

Here's why it works:

- Business credit bureaus (like D&B and Experian Biz) **report slowly**.

- Personal credit bureaus often **don't report business card balances** at all.

- That creates a window where you can apply to **multiple lenders at once**, maximizing approval odds.

This gives you **$50K–$150K+ in capital**, often at **0% interest for 12–18 months**—without showing up on your personal credit report.

---

**But Here's the Truth You Weren't Told**

**Business credit stacking is a chance to scale faster than most people ever will—but it's not a sacred grail.**
This is **leverage**—which means it multiplies results *in both directions.*

If your plan is solid and your income engine works, this capital can launch your freedom.

But if your plan fails and you can't repay, **you could face major consequences**:

- Damaged personal credit (if you gave a personal guarantee—which most do)

- Business credit wreckage

- Collections or lawsuits

- Years of cleanup

The banks want you to think it's just "free money."
It's not. It's a tool of the elite—and they use it **strategically, not emotionally.**

---

**How to Build and Stack Business Credit (Step-by-Step)**

1. **Form a Legit LLC**

   o Register it professionally with your state

   o Get an EIN (Employer Identification Number)

   o Set up a website, business email, and phone number

2. **Open a Business Bank Account**

   o Start establishing real banking relationships

3. **Build Early Business Credit**

   o Use vendors that report to D&B and Experian (Uline, NAV, etc.)

   o Pay on time, build a Paydex score

   o Get your DUNS number

4. **Apply for 3–5 Business Credit Cards Strategically**

   o Focus on cards with **0% intro APR**

   o Apply during a 1–2 week window before accounts report

   o Use banks that don't report business usage to personal credit (e.g., Chase, Amex, U.S. Bank)

---

**Example Business Credit Stack:**

| Bank | Card | 0% Intro | Limit Approved |
|------|------|----------|----------------|
| Chase | Ink Business Unlimited | 12 months | $20,000 |
| Amex | Blue Business Plus | 12 months | $25,000 |
| U.S. Bank | Triple Cash Rewards | 15 months | $15,000 |
| PNC | BusinessOptions Visa Signature | 13 months | $10,000 |

**Total: $70,000 in 0% capital.**

No impact on personal credit—**if used responsibly.**

---

### How Business Credit Affects Personal Credit

While most business credit cards **don't report usage or balances to personal credit bureaus,** they **still require a personal guarantee.**

That means:

- If you pay on time → **no impact**

- If you default or miss payments → **your personal credit *can* get wrecked**

Used right, this is clean leverage.
Used wrong, it's a financial landmine.

---

### What Can You Use It For?

- Fund paid ads or launch a product

- Buy inventory or outsource fulfillment

- Hire a team or scale operations

- Invest in a cash-flowing income asset

*But never use it to fund lifestyle or burn cash on hope.*
*It's fuel for systems, not a free roll.*

---

### Protecting Yourself:

- Always have a **clear plan** to deploy and repay before the 0% ends.

- Don't use this to fund *consumption*—only income-generating systems.

- Separate personal and business finances 100%.

- Use a **bookkeeper or CPA** to track it like a real business owner.

Business credit is a weapon. Use it wisely, and you scale like the elites.
Use it recklessly, and you're just another broke guy with a corporation.

**The 1% don't just access capital—they control it.**
That's the difference between scaling... and spiraling.

---

**Final Word on Risk and Reward**

**Business credit is leverage—not a lottery ticket.**
Treat it like investor capital. If your business fails and you can't repay, the debt follows *you*—not just the LLC.
This strategy is for builders, not gamblers.

Done right? It's how the rich scale with speed.
Done wrong? It's how dreamers go broke with $80K in business cards and nothing to show for it.

# Crypto, Gold, and Moving Value Outside the System

The system you live in wants one thing: **your money inside their walls.**

- In their banks
- In their retirement accounts
- In their inflated fiat
- In their tax jurisdiction

Because once your money is "in the system," it's **controlled, monitored, frozen, taxed, inflated, and devalued at will.**

The rich know this—and they've been quietly moving value off-grid for decades.

Now you're going to learn how.

---

### Why Move Value Outside the System?

Because if you don't **own it and control it**, you don't **really have it**.

Ask yourself:

- What happens if your bank freezes your account?
- What if your country inflates your savings into dust?
- What if your government limits withdrawals?
- What if capital controls lock your cash inside borders?

**These aren't conspiracy theories.** They're daily realities in over 50 countries—and the cracks are spreading everywhere.

The system is only stable if you're obedient.
But the moment you push for freedom? They show you the cage.

The solution? **Move value outside their reach.**

---

### 1. Gold – The Timeless Store of Sovereign Wealth

Gold is slow, heavy, and boring.
And that's exactly why the rich use it.

- It's **no one's liability**

- It holds purchasing power across centuries

- It's **outside the banking system**

- It's **private**, transportable, and globally accepted

You can:

- Hold physical gold in private vaults (domestic or offshore)

- Store in non-bank facilities (Brinks, SWP, etc.)

- Use tokenized gold (e.g. PAXG) for digital liquidity backed by physical metal

When governments collapse, currencies fail, or banking systems freeze—**gold buys you time, leverage, and safety.**

---

### ☐ 2. Crypto – The Digital Sovereign Weapon

Crypto isn't just an investment—it's a **freedom tool**.

- **Bitcoin** = decentralized, scarce, unconfiscatable money

- **Ethereum** = programmable finance

- **Stablecoins** = dollar value without bank dependency

- **Private wallets** = true self-custody

With crypto, you can:

- Send $10M across the world in minutes

- Hide wealth in a 12-word phrase

- Earn, borrow, and store value **without permission**

- Escape inflation, capital controls, and financial surveillance

Yes, crypto is volatile. Yes, there are scams.
But used correctly, it's **the single greatest financial exit ever created.**

The elite already use it:

- To hold digital liquidity

- To exit unstable systems

- To pass wealth privately across generations

It's not about "getting rich on coins"—it's about **owning the rails.**

---

### 3. Offshore + Multisystem Strategy

If you're playing a global game, you **don't keep everything in one country, currency, or system.**

The wealthy:

- Store assets in multiple jurisdictions

- Hold value in USD, CHF, BTC, gold, and real estate

- Use trusts, LLCs, and offshore corps to disconnect control from visibility

- Use **second residencies and digital citizenships** to escape traps

This gives them:

- Legal tax optimization

- Political risk insurance

- Financial resilience across currencies and borders

You don't need to flee your country.
But you **do** need to be able to **leave financially**—at any time.

---

**Warning: This Isn't About Hiding. It's About Freedom and Optionality**

This isn't about evasion. It's about **protection**.

- Protection from bad policy

- Protection from weaponized regulation

- Protection from the inevitable collapse of a fiat-driven, debt-sick system

If you want real freedom, you don't just make money.

You learn how to **move it, store it, protect it, and grow it—** outside their reach.

# Off-Grid Money Principles for Digital Freedom

What if you could:

- Earn money from anywhere

- Store wealth the system can't touch

- Operate without needing a bank

- Travel without borders or dependence

- Never worry about your country, your employer, or your government shutting you down

This isn't a dream. It's the **new playbook** of the digitally sovereign.

While most people are stuck in legacy systems, the rich and free are building **off-grid money ecosystems**—fully functional, highly mobile, and **outside traditional control.**

**Don't feel overwhelmed if some of this sounds advanced.**
You start with what you can control: building digital skills, creating independent income, and moving your first dollars outside the system.
This chapter isn't a to-do list—it's a **map of the terrain ahead**.
You're not behind. You're breaking out.

---

## 1. Earn Online, Globally, Anonymously

You don't need a job. You need **cash-flowing digital skill sets**:

- Freelancing (design, writing, editing, coding)

- Consulting, coaching, content

- Affiliate marketing, ecommerce, drop servicing

- Digital assets that earn while you sleep (courses, books, templates)

The goal?

**Income that isn't tied to a boss, a location, or a single platform.**

Get paid in:

- USD, EUR

- Stablecoins

- Crypto

- Barter or value exchange

Use platforms like:

- Upwork, Fiverr, Contra, Toptal

- Stripe, Wise, Payoneer (entry level)

- USDT/USDC wallet addresses (sovereign)

You don't just want money. You want **agile money.** Money that **moves with you**, not against you.

---

### 2. Escape Traditional Banks

Banks are slow. Surveillance-heavy. Fee-loaded. Vulnerable.

Start building a money stack that's **decentralized, layered, and flexible**:

- Hot wallets (Exodus, Trust, MetaMask) for daily use

- Cold storage (Ledger, Trezor) for long-term assets

- Multicurrency accounts (for bridge access)

- P2P networks for buying/selling without middlemen

- Use prepaid cards linked to stablecoins or offshore accounts

**Banks lock doors.**

Your system should be **liquid and borderless.**

---

**As your income grows, so should your infrastructure.**

You don't need offshore vaults and second passports on Day 1. But as you scale, the moves you once saw as distant will become necessary—and natural.

The goal isn't to be off-grid today. The goal is to be **unshakeable tomorrow.**

---

### 3. Structure for Survival and Growth

The more you earn, the more you need protection.
That means:

- LLCs or IBCs to handle business

- Trusts to hold long-term assets

- Foundations for legacy control

- Offshore corps for cross-border income

You don't just want money **flowing in**—you want it **routed smartly, hidden legally, and defended like treasure.**

This is what the rich do before they ever show wealth publicly.

---

### 4. Mobility = Power

If you can leave, they can't trap you.

That means:

- Second residency or passport (Panama, Mexico, Portugal, UAE, Paraguay)

- Offshore vaults or digital asset storage

- Exit plans for capital and citizenship

If your entire life is tied to one country—you're not free.
You're **hostage to policy.**

---

### The Off-Grid Money Mindset

- Control > Convenience

- Liquidity > Luxury

- Flexibility > Fame

- Optionality > Obedience

This isn't about going full prepper.
It's about **building systems that thrive in volatility**—so you don't just survive chaos, you **leverage it.**

---

The next recession, collapse, or lockdown will destroy those who only operate inside "the system."
But those who **own their income, their vaults, and their digital infrastructure?**
They'll be the new rulers of the free world.

# Chapter 6 – Multiplying Income Without Working Harder

## Scaling: The Real Trick of the Rich

Most people think making more money means:

- More hours

- More clients

- More grind

But the rich play a different game.

They don't earn more by working more.
They earn more by **multiplying output without multiplying effort.**

That's **scaling**—the real money lever.

Scaling isn't growth. Growth is effort-based. Scaling is **system-based**.
It's how you go from operator to **owner**, from labor to leverage.

Let's break it down.

---

### What Scaling Actually Means

Scaling means:

- Building systems that operate without you

- Multiplying the reach of your skill, product, or service

- Adding **layers of leverage** (people, code, capital)

It's what takes you from $5K/month solo freelancer...
To $50K/month agency owner
To $500K/year business operator
To $5M equity holder who doesn't touch daily ops.

---

## What Scaling Is *Not*:

- It's not "working faster"

- It's not hiring a bunch of VAs and micromanaging

- It's not throwing money at ads without infrastructure

**Scaling without systems = stress.**
**Scaling with systems = freedom.**

---

## The Scaling Cycle

1. **Do it yourself** – master the skill, validate the offer

2. **Document it** – turn your process into a repeatable system

3. **Delegate it** – hire or automate the repeatable parts

4. **Duplicate it** – across more clients, channels, or markets

5. **Detach from it** – become the owner, not the operator

This is how the rich stop trading time... and start buying time.

---

**You don't need to memorize tools or tactics here.**
What software to use, who to hire, which platform to automate—
those things change depending on your business.
What matters most—**the part you cannot skip or outsource**—is
that you deeply understand the **structure of scale**: systems, people,
and capital working together so you stop doing everything yourself.

Learn the concept now, and the specifics will follow. Miss it, and you'll stay stuck no matter how hard you work.

---

### The 3 Forces of Scale

### 1. People

You build a team—not to do what you hate, but to **amplify what you've proven works.**

- Contractors

- Agencies

- Internal hires

- Equity partners

You focus on **strategy and growth.** They execute.

### 2. Systems

If a process works, automate it.
From lead gen to fulfillment, use:

- CRMs, schedulers, auto-responders

- SOPs, automations, no-code tools

- AI assistants, Zapier flows, dashboards

Systems turn effort into **repeatable income.**

### 3. Capital

This is where it gets serious.

- You inject business credit (Chapter 5)

- You reinvest profits

- You partner with investors

- You fund **ads, assets, acquisitions**

Now your money multiplies money. That's when scale **explodes.**

---

### Scale Without Control = Death

If you scale chaos, you multiply burnout.
If you scale sloppy, you multiply problems.

**That's why poor entrepreneurs stay poor at higher revenue.**

Scaling **only works** when you have:

- A product or service that delivers real results

- A process you've proven works

- The discipline to stay out of your own way

---

### Final Word:

You've been taught to hustle harder.
The rich build machines.

Hustling gets you started.
**Scaling gets you freedom.**

And once you understand that, you'll never look at "more work" the same again.

# Passive Income Explained Simply

"Make money while you sleep."

You've heard the line.
You've seen the clickbait.

But most of what you've been told about passive income is either:

- Completely fake

- Technically true but functionally useless

- Or pitched by someone trying to sell you a course

Here's the real truth:

**Passive income is real—but it's not free, fast, or truly 100% passive.**
Even the most "automated" income streams need:

- Maintenance

- Monitoring

- Management

- Strategic input

The real win isn't *never working again*—it's **decoupling your income from your time**.
You stop being the machine. You own the machine.

Let's break down what it actually is, and how the rich create it on purpose.

## ✅ What Passive Income *Really* Means

Passive income is **money that continues to come in... after the upfront work is done.**

But that upfront work can involve:

- Time
- Capital
- Energy
- Systems
- Team

It's not "do nothing" money—it's **money detached from constant labor.**

Some income streams may feel 90% passive—like a rental property with a great property manager or a course that sells itself through a funnel.
But even those need occasional upgrades, oversight, and decisions. **The difference is, you control the inputs. You're not chained to the output.**

---

## Types of Passive Income

### 1. Capital-Based Passive Income

Your money is doing the work.

- Stock dividends
- Real estate cash flow
- REITs
- Lending income (P2P, crypto lending)

- Interest from notes or private deals

You need capital, patience, and positioning.

## 2. System-Based Passive Income

You built something that keeps working.

- Digital products (ebooks, courses, SaaS)

- Licensing intellectual property

- YouTube channels with monetized views

- Affiliate marketing systems

- Businesses with operators

You need to **build or buy the asset**, then **let the system do the heavy lifting**.

The rich usually do both.
They **build assets**, then **use capital to scale or acquire more**.

---

## What Passive Income Is *Not*

- Crypto pumping that depends on hype

- Buying a $1,000 course and calling it a business

- "Drop shipping" without knowing fulfillment

- Staking a coin and praying for moonshots

- Renting out your car and calling yourself retired

**If it needs you constantly managing, fixing, or worrying—it's not passive.**
If it dies the moment you stop?
It's not freedom—it's a trap.

**The Passive Income Formula**

Here's how the rich engineer it:

1. **Build a value machine** – Product, property, or platform that creates value

2. **Systemize delivery** – Automation, team, software, or outsourcing

3. **Redirect cash flow** – Into new assets or higher-leverage opportunities

4. **Protect it** – Legal structures, trusts, tax shields

5. **Repeat it** – Scale, stack, and diversify

Passive income isn't one stream—it's a **portfolio of controlled systems.**

---

**Final Word:**

The idea isn't to sit on a beach forever.

The goal is to **earn without being chained.**
To **own time**, not just money.
To **buy back your life**, one stream at a time.

# Systems, Automation, and Delegation

## How the Rich Build Income Machines That Don't Rely on Them

You don't get rich by doing more.
You get rich by doing **less of the right things**—and building machines to do the rest.

That's the difference between:

- The **operator** who works 12 hours a day to keep the business running

- And the **architect** who steps back, designs the system, and collects checks

The rich don't just build businesses. They build **engines**—and then **remove themselves from the driver's seat.**

Let's break down how they do it.

---

## 1. Systems: The Foundation of Scalable Money

A system is anything that:

- Produces consistent results

- Follows a repeatable process

- Can be mapped, tracked, or taught

If you do something more than twice, **systematize it**:

- Lead generation → automated funnel

- Client onboarding → templated sequence

- Sales calls → script and scheduler

- Delivery → SOP + software stack

Systems take what you're already doing—and make it **replicable without you.**

This is the **first step** in making income sustainable and scalable.

---

## 2. Automation: Remove Yourself from the Repetition

Once you have a system, you can plug in automation.
Now it runs 24/7, without asking you for anything.

Use tools like:

- Zapier, Make (Integromat), Pabbly → connect your apps

- Email autoresponders (ConvertKit, ActiveCampaign) → nurture leads

- Calendly → schedule without back-and-forth

- Stripe, PayPal, Gumroad → accept payments on autopilot

- AI tools → content, responses, lead handling

The goal is to **never touch something twice** if it can be done by tech.

The elite don't just automate for convenience.
They automate to **free mental bandwidth for high-leverage moves.**

---

## 3. Delegation: Install People Into the System

You're not supposed to do everything.
You're supposed to **design the workflow**—then give the execution to others.

Hire for:

- Repetitive tasks (admin, data entry, follow-up)

- Specialized skills (ads, editing, design)

- Operations (project managers, fulfillment teams)

- Growth (sales closers, SDRs, strategists)

Use platforms like:

- Upwork

- OnlineJobs.ph

- Agency partners

- Internal hires or contractors

You're not building an empire by yourself. You're building **through others**—with clarity, structure, and vision.

### The Final Level: Hire a System Manager

Once your systems are built and roles are delegated, your final move is to **hire someone to manage the team and operations for you.**

This could be:

- A general manager

- An operations lead

- A fractional COO

- A VA promoted into a systems coordinator

Their job:

- Ensure the team runs smoothly

- Manage task completion

- Solve routine problems

- Report KPIs and critical updates to you

**Your job becomes simple:** review metrics, make high-level decisions, and guide the machine—not run it.

Once you have this person in place and trust their judgment, you can reduce your check-ins to **once a week… then once a month.** You're no longer "self-employed." You're the **owner of a self-sustaining asset.**

---

**Most People Fail Because…**

- They refuse to let go

- They micromanage everything

- They have no documented process

- They think delegation means abdication

- They automate chaos instead of order

**Scaling trash = magnified failure.**
That's why the rich systematize **before** they scale.

---

**The Flow That Frees You:**

1. **Document** what you do

2. **Systemize** it into steps

3. **Automate** what can be done by tech

4. **Delegate** the rest to humans

5. **Review, optimize, repeat**

Now your business becomes a **machine**.
Your time shifts to **strategy, growth, and investing—not operations.**

---

You'll know you're winning when the money still moves… even when you don't.

# Turning Skills Into Scalable Assets

### The Rich Don't Just Use Skills—They Productize Them

The average person learns a skill…
Then sells it by the hour.
Forever.

The rich learn a skill, **package it into leverage**, and sell it to **hundreds, thousands, or millions**—without increasing effort.

That's the difference between:

- A freelancer writing copy for $500

- And a course creator teaching copywriting for $50,000/month

- And an agency owner scaling teams and systems to $500K/year

- And a licensing partner earning royalties from tools or frameworks they don't touch anymore

**Skills are the seeds. Assets are the trees.**
The rich grow trees. The broke sell seeds one by one.

---

### Step 1: Identify the Skill That Creates Results

You don't need to be a guru. You just need **a skill that solves a specific problem.** Something people would pay to shortcut, simplify, or succeed faster at.

It doesn't matter whether your skill is **digital, physical, local, or strategic**—if it creates value, it can be scaled.
What matters is that it solves a real problem, and that you stop trading it one hour at a time.

**Here's how that looks in the real world:**

✅ If you're a **copywriter**, you can sell messaging.

✅ If you're a **barber**, you can teach techniques or business growth.

✅ If you're into **car detailing**, you can package a system and teach others how to launch locally.

✅ If you're a **fitness coach**, you can sell training plans or meal systems.

✅ If you're a **dog trainer**, you can turn that process into an online course or a local licensing model.

✅ If you're a **chef**, you can build a digital cookbook with upsells into premium meal planning.

If your skill saves time, solves pain, or makes money—**it can be monetized.**

---

**Step 2: Package It Into Something That Scales**

The rich don't sell time. They **turn skills into scalable assets.**

Once you know your skill, ask:
*"How can I serve 100 people without working 100 hours?"*

That's where productization begins.

- A **copywriter** might launch a course on email strategy or sell templates.

- A **barber** could create a grooming masterclass and sell it worldwide.

- A **mechanic** might publish a tool guide or monetize repair tutorials.

117

- A **local chef** could build a membership around meal planning.

- A **dog trainer** might sell an online course *and* license their method to other trainers.

- A **contractor** could turn their estimate templates and process docs into a paid toolkit.

The method doesn't matter. The outcome does: **Your skill is no longer tied to your time.**

---

### Step 3: Distribute Through Leverage

You don't sell by calling people one by one.
You scale reach using:

- Paid ads

- Affiliates

- Organic content

- Email marketing

- Funnels

- Partnerships

- SEO

Now, **one skill** creates **many buyers**, and **one piece of content** sells **over and over.**

This is **real leverage**—not just talent, but **distribution.**

---

**Step 4: Systematize, License, or Exit**

Once the skill is productized and selling, you can:

- Delegate fulfillment (to a team or AI)

- License the IP (let others use your system under your brand)

- Sell the company or asset

- Turn it into evergreen income (set-and-forget digital product)

This is how skills become **cash-flowing assets**, then **equity plays**, then **legacy wealth.**

The broke work their skills.
The rich **monetize and multiply** them.

---

**Final Word:**

Every dollar you've ever made came from a skill.
But you were taught to trade that skill for money **one time only.**

Now you know the truth:

**You can turn that skill into something that pays you... forever.**

# Chapter 7 – The Inner Game of Money Domination

## Scarcity vs. Abundance Mindset

You can learn every tactic in this book.
You can use debt like a weapon, hide your income legally, stack business credit, and build scalable systems…

But if your **inner game is broken**, none of it will matter.

Because **how you think about money**—not just what you do with it—determines what you allow yourself to build, keep, and control.

---

### The Scarcity Mindset: The Default Operating System of the Poor and Middle Class

Scarcity is hardwired into you by:

- School

- Parents

- Media

- Employers

- Governments

It sounds like:

- "There's not enough."

- "If they win, I lose."

- "Rich people are greedy."

- "Money doesn't grow on trees."

- "It's not fair."

- "I'm just not wired for wealth."

And the most dangerous one:

**"I need to feel safe before I can take action."**

Scarcity makes you:

- Hoard cash instead of investing

- Undercharge because of fear

- Self-sabotage when things go well

- Envy others instead of learning from them

- Stay broke while feeling morally superior

Scarcity convinces you to worship security… and die poor inside a "safe" life.

But here's the truth:

**The system sold you fear so you'd never fight back.**
They want you scared, obedient, and small—because scared people don't build empires.
**Scared people don't study the game—they freeze.**
They stay stuck in "what if" while the bold are learning, building, and moving with intention.

**Every time you say "I can't afford that" instead of "how can I create that?"—you shrink.**
Scarcity is a virus. You either delete it or it dominates you.

**The Abundance Mindset: How the Rich Actually Think**

This isn't about fake affirmations or writing "I'm a money magnet" 20 times.

This is about a core belief:

**Money is unlimited if you learn how to create, control, and multiply value.**

Abundance sounds like:

- "If someone else is doing it, it means it's possible."

- "There's always another opportunity."

- "If I build something valuable, money will follow."

- "I can always rebuild if I lose it."

- "Money flows to power, control, and leverage—not effort."

Abundance lets you:

- Invest boldly

- Bet on yourself

- Learn from loss

- Act before you feel ready

- Collaborate instead of compete

Abundance creates the internal space to think long-term and act with power—even when it's scary.

And here's the difference:

**The rich don't wait for permission.**
They don't beg for stability. They create leverage, take shots, and build structures while everyone else is looking for certainty.

Abundance says:

**"I don't need guarantees—I need control."**
**"I'll risk short-term pain for long-term power."**
**"If I lose it all, I'll rebuild—faster, smarter, stronger."**

That's not mindset.

That's **mental armor.**
And you're going to need it if you want to dominate this game.

---

**How to Shift Permanently**

1. **Audit your money beliefs.**
   Write them out. Catch the programming. Who told you rich
   = evil? That you're "not that kind of person"? Burn it.

2. **Choose expansion over safety.**
   Scarcity asks "How can I protect what I have?"
   Abundance asks "How can I expand what I create?"

3. **Surround yourself with scalability.**
   Watch how rich people speak, act, build, and fail. Your
   environment is either feeding your fears—or showing you
   what's possible.

4. **Take action before you feel ready.**
   Scarcity wants certainty. Abundance trusts momentum.

---

**Final Word:**

You weren't born with a scarcity mindset.
You were programmed for it—so you could be controlled.

Break the code, and you stop thinking like a servant.
**Start thinking like a sovereign.**

# Why the Rich Don't "Feel Bad" About Wealth

You've been conditioned to feel guilty for wanting more.

- "Money changes people."

- "It's not about the money."

- "You should be grateful for what you have."

- "At least you have a job."

But guess what?

**The rich don't think like that. Not even close.**

They don't apologize for building power.
They don't shrink to make others feel comfortable.
They don't feel bad for dominating a system **they learned how to master.**

Because they understand something most people never figure out:

---

## Wealth Isn't Evil—It's a Tool

Money doesn't change who you are.
It **amplifies** who you are.

- If you're generous, it multiplies your impact.

- If you're strategic, it multiplies your influence.

- If you're lazy or entitled, it multiplies your delusion.

Wealth doesn't corrupt. **It exposes.**

The rich aren't scared of this—because they see money as a **neutral power source**. And they have **zero emotional baggage** around building more of it.

---

**Why You Feel Guilty—and Why It's a Trap**

Guilt around money is **programmed** into you:

- To keep you from asking for more

- To stop you from charging what you're worth

- To keep you in jobs that underpay and overuse you

- To make you **morally compliant while financially powerless**

If you feel bad for wanting wealth, you'll unconsciously sabotage it every time it gets close.

You'll say:

- "This is too much."

- "I'm not ready."

- "What will people think?"

- "Maybe I should give it away."

And the system wins—again.

**This is why your mindset is non-negotiable.**
Don't skim this part of the book. Don't treat it like a side note.

Because if your beliefs around money are broken, **every tactic you try will eventually break too.**

**Fix the code. Or stay trapped in the loop.**

---

**How the Rich Think Instead:**

- "I earned this."

- "I created value, so I deserve value."

- "If someone's offended by my success, they were never in my corner."

- "I can do more good with wealth than I ever could without it."

- "Money is a byproduct of power—and I'm here to build both."

The rich don't feel guilty for winning.
They feel **responsible** for protecting what they've built—and using it to create freedom.

They know:

**Being broke doesn't help anyone.**
**Staying small doesn't inspire anyone.**
**Feeling guilty doesn't change the world.**

---

**Final Word:**

You don't need to feel bad for wanting more.
You need to feel bad for **settling for less**.

Stop apologizing.
Stop shrinking.
**Build it. Keep it. Grow it.**
Because the system doesn't reward guilt.
It rewards **clarity, control, and action**.

# Mental Frameworks to Dominate the Long Game

**How the Rich Think Differently—Over Decades, Not Just Days**

The average person thinks in:

- Pay periods

- Tax seasons

- "Just get by this month" loops

The rich think in:

- Years

- Decades

- Legacy

- **Leverage across lifetimes**

The broke think: "How do I make $5K this month?"
The rich think: "How do I build an asset that prints $5K/month forever?"

Here's how you start making that shift—mentally, structurally, and strategically.

---

**Framework #1: The Owner's Mentality**

Stop thinking like a worker.
Stop thinking like a service provider.
Start thinking like an **owner**.

Ask:

- "Do I control this asset?"

- "Does this system work without me?"

- "Am I building something that scales, or just surviving?"

Owners think in cash flow, equity, and systems.
Employees think in tasks and hours.

---

### Framework #2: Play Long, Move Fast

Most people either:

- Think short-term and act impulsively
  **or**

- Dream long-term and never act at all

The rich do both:

- **They hold long-term vision** (freedom, scale, impact)

- **And execute fast, learn faster, and iterate without drama**

They don't wait for perfect.
They **move with speed, then refine with data.**

---

### Framework #3: Protect the Downside, Leverage the Upside

The rich aren't reckless.
They take big swings with **asymmetric risk:**

- Small downside

- Massive potential upside

How?

- They use **legal structures**

- They build in **cash buffers and income layers**

- They take **calculated bets**, not blind ones

They protect the castle first—**then go to war.**

---

## Framework #4: Data Over Drama

Poor thinkers ask, "How do I feel about this?"
Power thinkers ask, "What are the numbers telling me?"

Emotions lie.
**Data doesn't.**

- Track cash flow

- Know your ROI

- Watch the trends

- Let **feedback, not feelings** dictate your moves

The long game belongs to those who can stay calm and act on **truth**, not triggers.

---

## Framework #5: Compound Everything

This is the master key.

- Compound your skills

- Compound your assets

- Compound your network

- Compound your credibility

- Compound your control

What feels slow now will feel unstoppable later—**if you don't stop.**

Most people quit because growth looks invisible at first.
The rich **stay in the game long enough for the math to take over.**

---

Let's get real—**how badly do you actually want this?**
Is wealth just a casual thought you have while scrolling TikTok or sitting on the toilet?
Or is it a **full-blown mission** in your mind?

Because for the rich?
Wealth isn't a wish. It's a **company in their head**—always operating, always evolving, always demanding excellence.

Obsession? Yeah—**controlled obsession**. Not desperation.
Just a relentless drive to build freedom, power, and optionality—on purpose.

---

And here's a habit you need to install:
Everywhere you go—from the gym, to a restaurant, to the airport—ask yourself:
**"How does the money work here?"**

- Who owns this?

- What's the business model?

- What's being sold that isn't obvious?

- Where's the hidden leverage?

- **Is this even working?**

- **What would I fix or do better if this were mine?**

That's how future millionaires think.
They're not just **in the world**—they're **studying it**, decoding it, optimizing it, and eventually **buying pieces of it.**

---

**Final Word:**

Short-term thinking is how they trap you.
Long-term power is how you break out—and stay out.

The long game isn't about patience.
It's about **strategy backed by execution, fueled by relentless clarity.**

You're not just here to play the game.

**You're here to own the table.**

# Building Your Own Wealth Code

## Install the Thinking That Builds Empires

At this point, you've been exposed to:

- How the system traps you

- How the rich build power

- How to scale, protect, and multiply income

- How to think in decades, not days

- How to stop feeling bad for building wealth

- How to destroy scarcity and install sovereignty

Now it's time to **build your own wealth code**—the mental framework that guides every decision, filters every opportunity, and becomes **your compass for power.**

---

## What's a Wealth Code?

A **wealth code** is your personal philosophy, system, and structure around money, opportunity, and decision-making.

It's not one-size-fits-all.

It's the **OS in your head** that tells you:

- What to say yes to

- What to ignore

- What to build

- What to protect

- What to optimize

**What Your Wealth Code Should Include:**

1. **Your core belief about money**
   (Money flows to value and control—not effort)

2. **Your freedom metric**
   (e.g. $20K/month income from assets = total mobility and power)

3. **Your asset strategy**
   (e.g. cash flow first, then scale, then protect)

4. **Your time philosophy**
   (e.g. delegate early, protect deep work, say no to busy work)

5. **Your ethical compass**
   (e.g. win without exploitation, stay sovereign, help others escape)

6. **Your personal "hell no" list**
   (e.g. no W-2 jobs, no toxic clients, no time-for-money trap)

**Start Simple:**

You don't need a 30-page manifesto.

You need a clear internal command line that says:

**"This is what I build. This is how I move. This is who I become."**

Write your own code. Read it weekly. Refine it monthly.
Make every decision through its lens.

**Because if you don't run your own code—someone else's will run you.**

**Final Word:**

You're not just building wealth.
You're building a **philosophy, a strategy, and a system of self-rule.**

The broke chase money.
The rich install codes that print it.

And now, you're doing the same.

# Chapter 8 – Exit the System: Your Plan to Dominate

## What to Do With This Knowledge

Most people read something like this… and go back to scrolling.
Back to the job.
Back to "someday."
Back to the cage.

But not you.

If you've made it here, you're done waiting.
You're ready to exit the system—not just in theory, but in **execution.**

Here's what you need to understand:

---

### Information Alone Doesn't Free You—Implementation Does

This book isn't about "knowing."
It's about **unlearning, relearning, and applying under pressure.**

Power doesn't come from reading. It comes from **reconstruction.**
You tear out the broke scripts—and install a wealth operating system that works in the real world.

So what happens now?

---

**Step 1: Build Your Freedom Plan**

You need a tactical, personalized plan that matches your stage of the game.

Start simple:

- ✔ What's your current income?

- ✔ What's your monthly burn rate?

- ✔ What's your **Freedom Number**? (The amount you need monthly to be untouchable)

Then answer:

- How can I earn this number without a job?

- What skills or leverage vehicles can I scale now?

- How will I legally protect and multiply every dollar that comes in?

Put this in writing. Not in your head. Not as a dream.
**On paper, in a doc, or on a wall.**
It becomes your **operational directive**—not a wish.

---

Ask yourself:

- How much money can I **cut every week** to fund my freedom?

- What expenses are feeding comfort—but killing momentum?

- How many hours can I **steal back** from scrolling, bingeing, or wasting time to build instead?

Now go deeper:

- What skills do I need to learn to generate income outside the system?

- Do I need to buy a course—or can I start with free, tactical content?

- What would it take to **study 2 hours a day for 90 days**?

- What's the **first thing I can sell or produce** to make $500?

- What platform, tool, or system do I need to start building now?

Write your plan like this:

- Step 1: [Action] – [Time needed] – [Resources or cost]

- Step 2: [Action] – [Time needed] – [Resources or cost]

- Step 3: ...
  And so on—**until the escape is mapped.**

You don't need to be perfect. You need to **be precise and consistent.**

---

## Step 2: Act Like You're Already Free

You don't need permission to move like a builder, a sovereign, a strategist.

Start behaving like someone who's already out—even while you're transitioning:

- Make decisions based on **power**, not comfort

- Learn things that scale, not just entertain

- **Don't invest in image—invest in your ability to escape.**
  Flexing for strangers doesn't buy you freedom.
  Assets, skills, and systems do.

- Talk less. Execute more.

- Move like it's already real—because soon, it will be

**Your mindset has to arrive before your money does.**

---

### Step 3: Review, Refine, Repeat

No one builds freedom with one plan.
The elite review their game weekly, monthly, quarterly—**without emotion.**

Ask:

- What's working?

- What's wasting time?

- What can be automated or outsourced?

- What do I need to study, hire, or eliminate?

Freedom isn't a finish line. It's a system that stays sharp.
You don't just "exit once." You **re-exit constantly**—from old habits, bad thinking, broken systems, outdated strategies.

# Tools for Digital Freedom and Mobility

### The Software, Platforms, and Structures That Let You Move Like a Sovereign

You've built the mindset.
You've learned the strategies.
Now here's the **infrastructure** that makes it all work—on the move, under pressure, or outside the system.

---

### 1. Financial Tools to Store, Send, and Stack Value

These help you escape traditional banks and move money globally, privately, and efficiently.

- **Wise** – For multicurrency banking and international transfers

- **Revolut Business** – Clean interface for global income + spend

- **Crypto Wallets** – Trust Wallet, MetaMask, Exodus (hot wallets); Ledger, Trezor (cold wallets)

- **Stablecoins** – USDT, USDC (to store USD-equivalent value without a bank)

- **Curve / Plutus** – Spend crypto like fiat with linked cards

These aren't just alternatives—they're **escape hatches.**

---

## 2. Platforms to Earn Money from Anywhere

These tools let you earn income **regardless of location, employer, or traditional credentials**.

- **Upwork / Fiverr / Toptal** – Freelance platforms to monetize skills fast

- **Stripe / Gumroad / PayPal Business** – Accept payments globally

- **ConvertKit / ActiveCampaign** – Automate email-based business

- **Kajabi / Teachable / Podia** – Sell courses, digital products, and coaching

- **Beehiiv / Substack** – Launch paid newsletters (media as an asset)

These tools are how **side hustles turn into sovereign businesses.**

---

## 3. Mobility + Residency Infrastructure (Expanded)

Most people live their whole lives in one system—one passport, one tax code, one banking regime.
The rich don't.

They operate with **jurisdictional leverage.**

A second residency gives you:

✅ Legal backup if your home country turns hostile

✅ Access to foreign banking and investment

✅ Tax optimization opportunities

✅ The right to live, bank, and build somewhere else—**on your terms**

**And no—you don't have to be rich to get one.**

Countries like:

- **Paraguay** – low cost, permanent residency in months

- **Panama** – popular for U.S. citizens

- **Mexico** – 6-month visa-free, easy residency path

- **Estonia** – e-Residency lets you start a business in the EU without living there

- **Portugal, Georgia, UAE** – growing digital nomad and investor-friendly programs

**Example: Build Your Escape Option for ~$2,000**

1. Visit Paraguay on a tourist visa

2. File for permanent residency (no relocation required)

3. In 4–6 months, you're legally a resident—with access to banks, businesses, and second-country freedom

You don't have to leave your home country.
But you should always have **the legal ability to.**

Sovereignty starts with options.

---

### 4. Privacy + Sovereignty Tools (Expanded)

You don't need privacy tools because you're doing something wrong.
You need them because the system tracks, freezes, and taxes what it can see.

Most people expose everything:

- Emails scanned

- Payments tracked

- Files stored in Big Tech clouds

- Messages read

- Bank logins geo-tagged

The rich don't play like that.

**They protect identity, wealth, and communication at the source.**

**Starter Privacy Stack:**

- **ProtonMail / Tutanota** – Encrypted email for sensitive accounts

- **Mullvad / Proton VPN** – No-log, anonymous browsing (no email required to sign up)

- **Skiff / CryptPad** – Private cloud storage with encryption

- **Obsidian / Notion (local)** – Build a private wealth strategy doc that lives offline

- **Signal / Session / SimpleX** – Messaging that can't be intercepted or logged

Total setup time: ~2 hours
Total impact: **Untrackable control.**

The less exposed you are, the harder you are to censor, freeze, or manipulate.

---

**Final Word:**

These are your levers. Your switches. Your infrastructure.

Use them to build.
Use them to earn.
Use them to move quietly, powerfully, and independently.

You're not just escaping a job.
You're exiting a system.

And these are the tools that keep you free **once you're out.**

## Let's get one thing straight:

If your belief isn't absolute, it's useless.

You either **know you're going to dominate this game**, or you're living in *maybe-land*.
And *maybe* is where success goes to die.

"Maybe I'll start a business."
"Maybe I'll learn sales."
"Maybe I'll build something next year."

**Maybe means you're not serious.**
It means you're still waiting for proof, permission, or a push that will never come.

But here's the shift:
You don't need a new personality.
You don't need a trust fund.
You need to flip the internal switch from:

"Maybe I could" → **"I must—and I will."**

Because when it becomes non-negotiable, you stop hesitating.
You find the time.
You find the money.
You find the answer.
You stop scrolling. You start building.
You stop asking. You start moving.

This isn't about reckless action.
It's about **relentless certainty**.
Certainty builds action. Action builds escape.

Now. With what you've got.
Because your freedom depends on it.

# Final Words

You've just read the kind of book they never wanted you to find.

Not because it's illegal.
But because it's **dangerous**—to the system that profits from your obedience.

Now you know how the 1% play the game.
More importantly, you know **how to beat them at it.**

You've seen:

- How the system is rigged

- How wealth is built and protected

- How the rich move, think, and dominate

- How to turn skills into assets

- How to exit the trap—**for good**

But knowledge alone won't save you.

You either become the kind of person who acts on what they know…
Or you stay the kind who just "knows things" and keeps losing.

**They lied to you.**
They trained you to obey, to shrink, to stay broke and be grateful for it.

**This book is your revenge.**
Not with fists—but with freedom.
Not with noise—but with results.
Not by complaining—but by *owning everything they said you'd never have.*

**Success is the best revenge.**
And now, you're holding the trigger.

So here's my challenge:

**Close this book—and make your next move the one that breaks the cycle.**

Because no one's coming to save you.
But now, you don't need them.